Guitar • Vocal

H★MILTON

AN AMERICAN MUSICAL BY LIN-MANUEL MIRANDA

ISBN 978-1-4950-8838-4

EXCLUSIVELY DISTRIBUTED BY

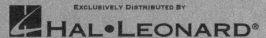

Visit Hal Leonard Online at
www.halleonard.com

Contact us:
Hal Leonard
7777 West Bluemound Road
Milwaukee, WI 53213
Email: info@halleonard.com

In Europe, contact:
Hal Leonard Europe Limited
42 Wigmore Street
Marylebone, London, W1U 2RN
Email: info@halleonardeurope.com

In Australia, contact:
Hal Leonard Australia Pty. Ltd.
4 Lentara Court
Cheltenham, Victoria, 3192 Australia
Email: info@halleonard.com.au

Alexander Hamilton

Words and Music by
Lin-Manuel Miranda

(Capo 2nd fret)

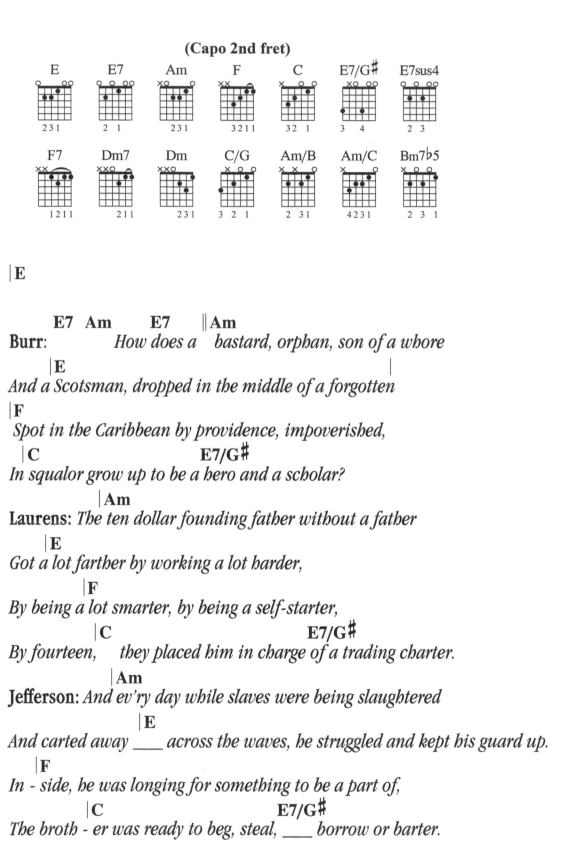

Intro |E

Verse 1
                 E7 Am   E7 ||Am

Burr: *How does a   bastard, orphan, son of a whore*

|E |

And a Scotsman, dropped in the middle of a forgotten

|F

Spot in the Caribbean by providence, impoverished,

 |C   E7/G♯

In squalor grow up to be a hero and a scholar?

               |Am

Laurens: *The ten dollar founding father without a father*

    |E

Got a lot farther by working a lot harder,

      |F

By being a lot smarter, by being a self-starter,

        |C   E7/G♯

By fourteen,   they placed him in charge of a trading charter.

            |Am

Jefferson: *And ev'ry day while slaves were being slaughtered*

                |E

And carted away ____ across the waves, he struggled and kept his guard up.

 |F

In - side, he was longing for something to be a part of,

        |C   E7/G♯

The broth - er was ready to beg, steal, ____ borrow or barter.

Verse 2

        ‖ **Am**
Madison: *Then a hurricane came, and devastation reigned,*

    |**E**
Our man ___ saw his future drip, dripping down the drain,

  |**F**
Put a pencil to his temple, connected it to his brain,

    |**C**   **E7sus4**   **E7/G♯**
And he wrote his first refrain, a tes - tament to his pain.

          |**Am** |
Burr: Well, the word got around, they said, "This kid is insane, man."

|**E** |
 Took up a collection just to send him to the mainland.

|**F**
"Get your education, don't forget from whence you came,

    |**C**   **E7/G♯**   ‖
And the world is gonna know your name.   What's your name, man?"

Verse 3

         ‖ **Am** |**E**
Hamilton: Alexander Hamilton. My name is Alexander Hamilton.

        |**F**
And there's a million things I haven't done,

      |**C**   **E7/G♯**
But just you wait, just you ___ wait…

Verse 4

          ‖ **Am**
Eliza: When he was ten his father split, full of it, debt ridden,

         |**E**
Two years ___ later, see Alex and his mother bedridden,

       |**F**
Half - dead sittin' in their own sick, the scent thick,

                            |**N.C.** |
All (minus Hamilton): *And Alex got better but his mother went quick.*

          |**Am** |
Washington: Moved in with a cousin, the cousin committed suicide.

|**E**
 Left him with nothin' but ruined pride, something new inside,

 |**F**
A voice sayin "Alex, You gotta fend for yourself."

      |**C**   **E**
He started retreatin' and readin' ev'ry treatise on the shelf.

Verse 5

‖Am   N.C.

Burr: *There would have been nothin' left to do for someone less astute,*

    |E   N.C.

He woulda been dead or destitute without a cent of restitution,

   |F   N.C. |

Started workin',   clerkin' for his late mother's landlord,

|C   E7/G♯   ‖

Tradin' sugarcane and rum and all the things he can't afford.

Verse 6

‖Am |E

Scammin' for every book he can get his hands on, plannin' for the future,

                    |F

See him now as he stands on the bow of a ship headed for a new land.

 |C   E7/G♯

In New York you can be a new man.

Verse 7

‖Am

In New York, you can be a new man.

            Hamilton: Just you wait!

 |F7

In New York, you can be a new man.

             Just you wait!

 |Dm7

In New York you can be a new man,

 |E7sus4   N.C.   E7/G♯   ‖

In New York! New York!

           Just you wait!

Verse 8

```
              ‖ Am
```
Burr/Mulligan/Laurens: Alexander Hamilton, Alexander Hamilton.

```
        | F7
```
We are waiting in the wings for you. Waiting in the wings for you.

                                                                       You could

```
| Dm7                                           | E7sus4  N.C.
```
 Never back down, you never learned to take your   time!

```
E7/G♯ | Am                                        | F7
```
     Oh, Alexander Hamilton, Alexander Hamilton, A - merica sings for you,

```
                              | Dm7
```
Laurens/Mulligan: Will they know what you overcame?

```
               | Am               Dm
```
Will they know ___ you rewrote the game?

```
        | Am        Dm    | C/G         E7/G♯
```
The world ___ will nev - er be ___ the same, ___ oh…

Verse 9

```
               ‖ Am                     Am/B                 |
```
Burr: The ship is in the harbor now, see if you can spot him.

```
| Am/C                    Dm7
```
     Another immigrant, com - in' up from the bottom,

```
     | F                         | Bm7♭5            |
```
His enemies destroyed his rep, A - merica forgot him…

```
                                          | E7sus4      E7
```
Mulligan/Madison/Lafayette/Jefferson: *We fought with him.*

```
               E7sus4       E7          | Am              E7
```
Laurens/Philip: *Me? I died for him.* **Washington**: *Me? I trusted him.*

```
                          Bm7♭5              E        |
```
Eliza/Angelica/Peggy/Mariah: *Me? I loved him.* **Burr**: *And Me?*

```
| Bm7♭5  N.C.                       | E
```
    I'm the damn fool that shot him. (Shot him. Shot him.)

```
                  | F                      C          | Bm7♭5
```
Ensemble: There's a million things I haven't done, __ but just you wait!

```
     E7        Am    E7        | N.C.                Am ‖
```
Burr: What's your name, man? **Ensemble**: Alexander Hamilton!

My Shot

Words and Music by LIN-MANUEL MIRANDA
with Albert Johnson, Kejuan Waliek Muchita, Osten Harvey, Jr.,
Roger Troutman, Christopher Wallace

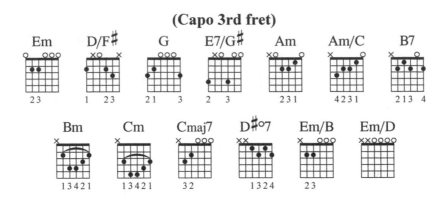

(Capo 3rd fret)

Chorus 1

|Em   D/F#
Hamilton: *I am not throwing away my shot!*

|G
I am not throwing away my shot!

E7/G# |Am
Hey yo, I'm just like my country, I'm young, scrappy and hungry,

    |Am/C   B7
And I'm not throwing away my shot!

Verse 1

      ||Em
Hamilton: *I'm 'a get a scholarship to King's College.*

           D/F# |G
I prob'bly should - n't brag, but dag, I amaze and astonish.

       E7/G# |Am
The problem is I got a lot of brains but no polish.

    Bm |Cm N.C.
I gotta hol - ler just to be heard. With every word, I drop knowledge!

Verse 2

|| **Em**
Hamilton: *I'm a diamond in the rough,*
              D/F♯ |**G**
A shiny piece of coal ___ tryin' to reach my goal.
                      E7/G♯ |
My power of speech: unimpeach - able.
|**Am**
 Only nineteen but my mind is old - er.
  |**Am/C**   **B7**
These New York city streets get cold - er,
             |**Em**   **D/F♯**
I shoulder ev'ry burden, ev'ry disadvantage I have learned to man - age,
      |**G**
I don't have a gun to brandish, I walk these streets famished.
  |**Am**
The plan is to fan this spark into a flame.
  |**Am/C**   **B7**
But damn, it's getting dark, so let me spell out the name,
                         |**Em**   **D/F♯**|**G**
I am the **Hamilton/Laurens/Lafayette/Mulligan**: *A-L-E-X-A-N-D -*   *E-R.*
              |**Am**
We are meant to be a **Hamilton**: *col - ony that runs independently.*
    |**Am/C**   **B7**
Meanwhile Britain keeps shittin' on us endlessly.
   |**Em**
Essen - tially, they tax us relentlessly,
D/F♯ |**G**   **E7/G♯**
Then King George turns around, runs a spending spree.
     |**Am**
He ain't ever gonna set his descendents free,
    |**Am/C**   **B7**
So there will be a revolution in this century.
 |**N.C.**   **Em**   **D/F♯**
En - ter me! **Mull/Laur/Laf**: *(He says in parentheses.)*
           |**G**   **E7/G♯**
Hamilton: *Don't be shocked when your hist'ry book mentions me.*
   |**Am**
I will lay down my life if it sets us free.
      |**Am/C**   **B7** ||
Even - tually, you'll see my as - cendancy. And I am...

Chorus 2

                ‖**Em**   **D/F♯**

Hamilton: *Not throwing away my shot.*

  |**G**

I am not throwing away my shot.

   E7/G♯ |**Am**

Hey yo, I'm just like my country, I'm young, scrappy and hungry,

    |**Am/C**   **B7**   **E7/G♯**

And I'm not throwing away my   shot.   I am

               |**Em**   **D/F♯**

Hamilton/Laurens: *not throwing away my shot.*

  |**G**

I am not throwing away my shot.

   E7/G♯ |**Am**

Hey yo, I'm just like my country, I'm young, scrappy and hungry,

    |**Am/C**   **B7**

And I'm not throwing away my   shot.

Verse 3

    ‖**Em**   **D/F♯** |
It's time to take a shot! **Layfayette**: *I dream of life without a monarchy.*

|**G**   **E7/G♯** |
The unrest in France will need to 'on - archy?

|**Am** |
'Onarchy? How you say, how you say, "anarchy?"

|**Am/C**   **B7** |**Em**
When I fight, I made the other side panicky with my shot!

                           D/F♯
Mulligan: *Yo, I'm a taylor's appren - tice,*

  |**G**   **E7/G♯**
And I got y'all knuckleheads in loco paren - tis.

  |**Am**
I'm joining the rebellion 'cause I know it's my chance

    |**Am/C**   **B7**
To social - ly advance, instead of sewin' some pants!

       |**Em**   **D/F♯**
I'm gonna take a shot! **Laurens**: *But we'll never be truly free*

  |**G**   **E7/G♯**
Un - til those in bondage have the same rights as you and me,

   |**Am**
You and I. Do or die.

                  |**Am/C**   **B7**
Wait till I sally in on a   *stallion with the first black battalion.*

     |**Em**   **D/F♯**
Have an - other shot! **Burr**: *Geniuses, lower your voic - es.*

  |**G**   **E7/G♯**
You keep out of trouble and you double your choic - es.

  |**Am**
I'm with you, but the situation is fraught.

    |**Am/C**   **B7** | **Em**
You've got to be carefully taught: ___ if you talk, you're gonna get shot!

                         D/F♯
Hamilton: *Burr, check what we got.*

    |**G**
Mister Lafayette, hard rock like Lancelot,

E7/G♯ |**Am**
I think your pants look hot, Laurens, I like you a lot.

    |**Am/C**   **B7**
Let's hatch a plot blacker than the kettle callin' the pot…

       |**Em**
What are the odds the gods would put us all in one spot,

D/F♯ |**G**
Poppin' a squat on conventional wisdom, like it or not,

E7/G♯ |**Am** |
A bunch of revolutionary manumission abolitionists?

|**N.C.**   ‖
Give me a position, show me where the ammunition is!

Verse 4

‖ N.C.

Hamilton: *Oh, am I talkin' too loud?*

|

Sometimes I get over excited, shoot off at the mouth.

| |

I never had a group of friends before, I promise that I'll make y'all proud.

|

Laurens: *Let's get this guy in front of a crowd.*

Chorus 3

‖ **Em**

Ensemble: I am not throwing away my shot.

D/F♯ |**G**

I am   not throwing away my shot.

   E7/G♯ |**Am**

Hey yo, I'm   just like my country, I'm young, scrappy and hungry,

        |**Am/C**   **B7**

And I'm not throwing away my   shot.

     |**Em**

I am not throwing away my shot.

D/F♯ |**G**

I am   not throwing away my shot.

     E7/G♯ |**Am**

Hey yo,   I'm just like my country, I'm young, scrappy and hungry,

        |**Am/C**   **B7**   ‖

And I'm not throwing away my shot. **Laurens:** *Ev'rybody sing:*

Bridge

                    ‖ **Em** |

Laur/Ham/Laf/Mull: Whoa, whoa, whoa!

|**G** |**Cmaj7** |

   Hey! Whoa! _____ *Wooh!* Whoa!

          |**B7** |

Laurens: *Ay, let 'em hear ya! Let's go!*

          |**Em**

Ensemble: Whoa, whoa, whoa!

                   |**G** |

Laurens: *I said, shout it to the rooftops!* Ensemble: Whoa!

       |**Cmaj7** |

Laurens: *Said, to the rooftops!* Ensemble: Whoa!

       |**D♯°7**   **B7**   ‖

Laurens: *Come on!* Ensemble: Yeah! ___ Laurens: *Come on, let's go!*

Verse 5

       ‖ **Em**   **D/F♯** |**G**

Laurens: Rise up! When you're living on your knees, ___ you rise up.

                       |**Cmaj7**

Tell your brother that he's gotta rise up.

                       |**D♯°7**

Tell your sister that she's gotta rise up.

                    B7 |**Em**

Laur/Laf/Mull+Ens: *When are these colonies gonna rise up?*

                     D/F♯ |**G**

When are these colonies ___ gonna rise up?

                    E7/G♯ |**Am**

When are these colonies ___ gonna rise up?

                    |**Am/C**   **B7**

When are these colonies gonna rise up? *Rise up!*

Verse 6

             ‖ **Em**

Hamilton: *I imagine death so much it feels more like a memory.*

           |**G**

When's it gonna get me? In my sleep? Seven feet ahead of me?

|**Cmaj7**

*   If I see it comin', do I run or do I let it be?*

|**B7**

* Is it like a beat without a melody?*

         |**Em**

See, I never thought I'd live past twenty.

         |**G**

Where I come from some get half as many.

        |**Cmaj7**

Ask anybody why we livin' fast and we laugh, reach for a flask,

|**B7**   ‖

We have to make this moment last, that's plenty.

Verse 7

    ‖ **Em**   **D/F♯** |

Hamilton: *Scratch that, this is not a moment, it's a move - ment*

|**G** |

Where all the hungriest brothers with something to prove went.

|**Cmaj7** |

Foes oppose us, we take an honest stand,

|**B7** |

We roll like Moses, claimin' our promised land.

|**Em**   **D/F♯** |

And? If we win our indepen - dence?

|**G** |

'Zat a guarantee of freedom for our descendants?

|**Cmaj7** |

Or will the blood we shed begin an endless

|**B7**   ‖

Cycle of vengeance and death with no defendants?

Verse 8

    |**Em**

Hamilton: *I know the action in the street is excitin',*

      |**G** |

But Jesus, between all the bleedin' 'n' fightin' I've been readin' 'n' writin'.

|**Am** |

We need to handle our financial situation.

|**Am/C**   **B7** |

Are we a nation of states? ____ What's the state of our nation?

|**Em**

I'm past patiently waitin'.

          D/F♯ |**G**   **E7/G♯** |

I'm passionate - ly smashin' ev'ry expectation, ev'ry action an act of creation.

|**Am**

I'm laughin' in the face of casualties and sorrow,

  |**B7**   **N.C.**

For the first time, I'm thinkin' past tomorrow.

Chorus 4

          B7   **‖Em**

Ensemble: And I am not throwing away my shot.

D/F♯ | **G**

I am   not throwing away my shot.

    E7/G♯ | **Am**

Hey yo, I'm   just like my country, I'm young, scrappy and hungry,

      | **Am/C**   **B7**

And I'm not throwing away my   shot.

                           | **Em**

We're gonna **Ham/Laur/Laf/Mull**: *Rise up!*   *Time to take a shot!*

Ensemble: Not throwing away my   shot!

                   D/F♯ | **G**

Ham/Laur/Laf/Mull: *We're gonna rise up!*   *Time to take a shot!*

Ensemble   Not throwing away my   shot.

           E7/G♯ | **Am** |

Ensemble: We're gonna   rise up! Rise up!

Hamilton: *It's time to take a shot!*

     | **Em/B** |

Ensemble: Rise up! Rise up!

Ham/Laur/Laf/Mull: *It's time to take a shot!*

     | **Am/C** |

Ensemble: Rise up!

Ham/Laur/Laf/Mull: *It's time to take a shot!* **Ensemble**: Rise up!

            | **Em/D**

Ham/Laur/Laf/Mull: *Take a shot! Shot! Shot!*

     | **B7**

A-yo, it's time to take a shot! Time to take a shot!

    | | **Em N.C.** ‖

And I am not throwing away my, not throwing away my shot!

You'll Be Back

Words and Music by
Lin-Manuel Miranda

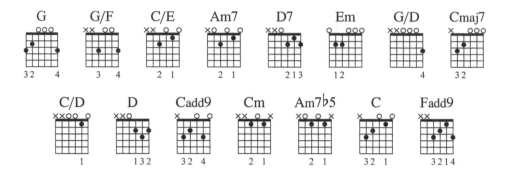

Intro |G |G/F |C/E |

Verse 1
|Am7 D7 |G |G/F

King George: You say ___ the price of my love's
|C/E |
Not a price ___ that you're willing to pay.
|Am7 D7 |G |G/F |
You cry ___ in your tea ___ which you hurl in the sea
|C/E |Am7   D7 |Em
When you see me go by. ___ Why ___ so sad?
|G/D |Cmaj7 |C/D
Re - member we made an arrange - ment when you went away,
D |Em
Now you're making me mad.
|G/D |Cadd9 |C/D
Re - member, despite our estrange - ment, I'm your man.

Verse 2

```
N.C.              ‖ G              |G/F
```
You'll be back.   Soon you'll see.
```
                  |C/E                      |
```
You'll remem - ber you belong to me.
```
|Am7      D7              |G              |G/F
```
   You'll ___ be back. ___ Time will tell.
```
                  |C/E                      |
```
You'll remem - ber that I served you well.
```
|Am7  D7          |Em              |G/D
```
   O - ceans rise, ___ empires fall,
```
                  |Cmaj7                  |Cm
```
We have seen ___ each other through it all,
```
                  |Em              |G/D
```
And when push ___ comes to shove,
```
      |Cadd9                  |C/D              D          ‖
```
I will send a fully armored battal - ion to remind you of my…

Chorus 1

```
              ‖G                  |G/F                  |
```
   Love! Da, da, da, dat, da, ___ dat, da, da, da,
```
|C/E                  |Am7♭5      D7              |
```
 Da, ya, da, da, da, dat,   dat, da, ___ ya, da!
```
|G                      |G/F                  |
```
    Da, da, da, dat, da, ___ dat, da, da, da,
```
|C/E                  |Am7♭5      D7
```
 Da, ya, da, da, da, dat,   dat, da.

Bridge

```
      ‖ Em          |G/D                      |Cmaj7      |
```
You say our love is draining and you can't go on.
```
|Cm      |Em              |G/D              |C      |
```
    You'll be the one com - plaining when I am gone.
```
|Cm   |Am7                      |D
```
   And no, don't change the sub - ject
```
      |Am7                  |D
```
'Cause you're my fav'rite sub - ject.
```
      |Fadd9              |Cmaj7
```
My sweet, submissive sub - ject,
```
      |Fadd9      |Cmaj7
```
My loyal, royal sub - ject,
```
      |G      |G/F   |Cm              |
```
For - ever and ever and ever and ever and ever.

Verse 3

```
N.C.                ‖ G          | G/F
You'll be back,        like be - fore.
                   | C/E                                |
I will fight ____ the fight and win the war
| Am7    D7            | G
   For ____ your love,
                           | G/F          | C/E                      |
For your praise, ____ and I'll love ____ you till my dying days.
| Am7       D7            | Em             | G/D
   When ____ you're gone ____ I'll go mad,
                   | Cmaj7                     | Cm
So don't throw ____ away this thing we had.
                       | Em            | G/D
'Cause when push ____ comes to shove
                   | Cadd9                        | C/D              ‖
I will kill ____ your friends and family to re - mind you of my love.
```

Chorus 2

```
‖ G                      | G/F                  |
   Da, da, da, dat, da, ____ dat, da, da, da,
| C/E                | Am7♭5        D7              |
 Da, ya, da, da, da, dat,      dat, da, _____ ya, da!
| G                      | G/F                  |
   Da, da, da, dat, da, ____ dat, da, da, da,
| C/E                | Am7♭5           D7       ‖
 Da, ya, da, da, da, dat,     dat. *Every - body!*
```

Outro-Chorus

```
‖ G                      | G/F                  |
   Da, da, da, dat, da, ____ dat, da, da, da,
| C/E                | Am7♭5        D7              |
 Da, ya, da, da, da, dat,      dat, da, ____ ya, da!
| G                       | G/F | C/E                  |
   Da, da, da, dat, da, _____ ya, da, da, da, da, da
| Am7♭5  D7   | G           |           ‖
 Dat, dat,  da, ya, da.
```

Wait for It

Words and Music by
Lin-Manuel Miranda

(Capo 1st fret)

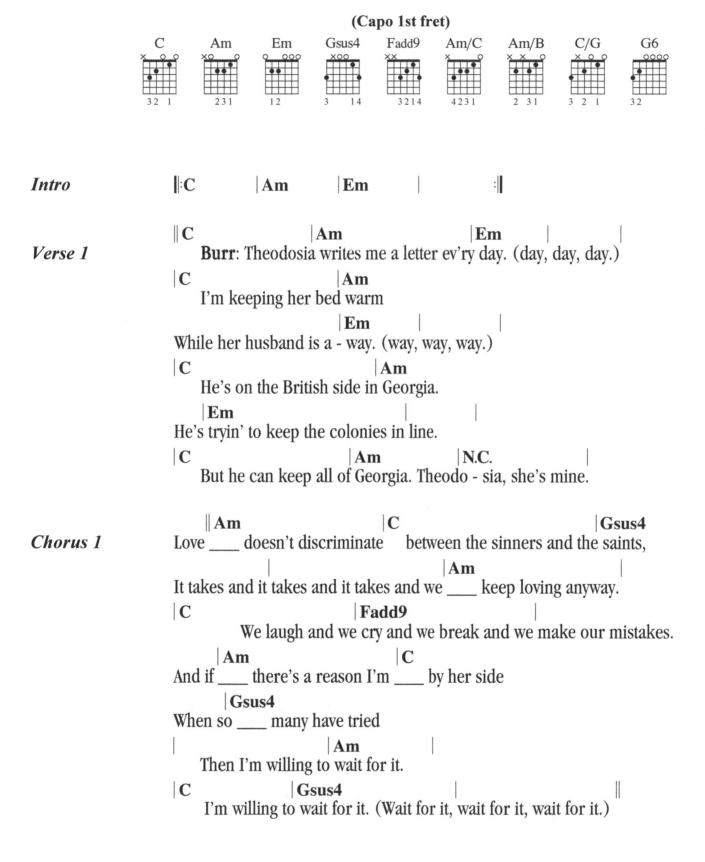

Intro

‖: C | Am | Em | | :‖

Verse 1

‖ C | Am | Em | |
Burr: Theodosia writes me a letter ev'ry day. (day, day, day.)

| C | Am
I'm keeping her bed warm

| Em | |
While her husband is a - way. (way, way, way.)

| C | Am
He's on the British side in Georgia.

| Em | |
He's tryin' to keep the colonies in line.

| C | Am | N.C. |
But he can keep all of Georgia. Theodo - sia, she's mine.

Chorus 1

‖ Am | C | Gsus4
Love ____ doesn't discriminate   between the sinners and the saints,

| | Am |
It takes and it takes and it takes and we ____ keep loving anyway.

| C | Fadd9 |
We laugh and we cry and we break and we make our mistakes.

| Am | C
And if ____ there's a reason I'm ____ by her side

| Gsus4
When so ____ many have tried

| | Am |
Then I'm willing to wait for it.

| C | Gsus4 | ‖
I'm willing to wait for it. (Wait for it, wait for it, wait for it.)

Verse 2

```
        ‖C                               |Am                    |Em
Burr:       My grandfather was a fire and brimstone preacher,
                |                           |
Ensemble: Preacher, preacher, preacher.
        |C                               |Am                        |Em
Burr:       But there are things that the homilies and hymns won't teach ya.
                |                           |
Ensemble: Teach ya, teach ya, teach ya.
        |C                       |Am
Burr:       My mother was a genius,
 |Em                    |                                   |C
My father commanded re - spect. Ensemble: Respect, re - spect.
                                |Am                    |
Burr: When they died they left ___ no instructions.
|N.C.                            |
        Just a legacy to pro - tect.
```

Chorus 2

```
        ‖Am                          |C                          |Gsus4
Death ___ doesn't discriminate     between the sinners and the saints,
                |                            |Am                    |
It takes and it takes and it takes and we ___ keep living anyway.
|C                      |Fadd9                  |
     We rise and we fall and we break and we make our mistakes.
        |Am                      |C
And if ___ there's a reason I'm ___ still alive
        |Gsus4                      |                |Am            |
When everyone who loves me has died I'm willing to wait for it.
|C              |N.C.          |            ‖
     I'm willing to wait for it.
```

Verse 3

```
        ‖Am                    |                    |
Burr: Wait for it.
        Wait for it, wait for it, wait for it, Wait for it.
|C                          |                |Am
     I am the one thing in life I can con - trol.
                                    ‖: Wait for it, wait for it, :‖
|Fadd9              |              |Am                  |
I am inimitable,   I am an original.
                                    ‖: Wait for it, wait for it, :‖
|C                      |              |Am                  |
I'm not falling be - hind or running late.
                                    ‖: Wait for it, wait for it, :‖
|Fadd9 N.C.          |        Fadd9      ‖
I'm not standing still, I am lying in…
```

Verse 4

```
‖Am          |              |
  Wait.
         Wait, wait, wait.
|C              |           |Am        |            |
 Hamilton faces an endless uphill climb.
                              Climb, climb, climb.
 |Fadd9            |              |Am      |          |
  He has something to prove, he has nothing to lose.
                                   Lose, lose, lose.
|C                 |              |Am       |         |
 Hamilton's pace is re - lentless, he wastes no time.
                                Time, time, time.
 |Fadd9           |
  What is it like in his shoes?
```

Verse 5

```
|       ‖C            |Am              |Em
  Ham - ilton doesn't hesitate.    He exhibits no re - straint.
            |                   |C
He takes and he takes and he ___ keeps winning anyway.
|Am           |Em              |
  He changes the game. He plays and he raises the stakes.
    |Am              |Am/C
And if ___ there's a reason he ___ seems to thrive
      |Am/B                |
When so ___ few survive, then God - damn it,
           |Am      |C         |Fadd9         |
I'm willing to wait for it.    I'm willing to wait for it.
```

Chorus 2

```
   ‖Am                   |C                    |Gsus4
Life ___ doesn't discriminate    between the sinners and the saints,
          |                   |Am                        |
It takes and it takes and it takes.
                           And we ___ keep living anyway.
|C            |Fadd9          |      |Am
  We rise ___ and we fall, ___ and if ___ there's a reason
     |C              |C/G           |G6
I'm ___ still alive when so ___ many have died,    then I'm willing to…
```

Outro

```
|C   |Am  |Em          |                        |C
           Burr: Wait for it. Ensemble: Wait for it. Wait for it.
     |Am                  |Em
Burr: Wait for it. Ensemble: Wait for it. Wait for it. Wait for it.
   |              |              |C         ‖
Wait for it. Wait for it. Wait for it. Wait for it. Wait.
```

That Would Be Enough

Words and Music by
Lin-Manuel Miranda

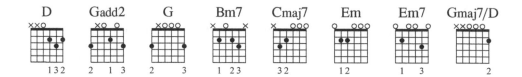

Intro |D |Gadd2 G ‖

Verse 1

|D |Bm7 |

Eliza: Look at where you are. Look at where you started.

|D |

The fact that you're alive is a miracle.

|G Gadd2 |

Just stay alive, ____ that would be enough.

|D |Bm7 |D

And if this child ____ shares a fraction of your smile

|G

Or a fragment of your mind,

Gadd2 ‖

Look out, world! ____ That would be enough.

Verse 2

‖D |Bm7 |D

I don't pretend to know ___ the challenges you're fac - ing.

                             |Cmaj7   Em |D

The worlds you keep eras - ing and creating in ___ your mind.

          |Bm7 |

But I'm not afraid.   I know who I married.

|D |G

   So long as you come home at the end of the day,

Gadd2   ‖

   That would be enough.

Verse 3

‖D |Bm7 |D

   We don't need a legacy. ___ We don't need money.

                        |Gadd2

If I could grant you peace of mind.

                     |Bm7

If you could let me inside your heart…

                  |Em7 |Bm7

Oh, let me be a part of the narrative in the story they will write some - day.

                  |Em7

Let this moment be the first chapter

          |Bm7 |

Where you decide to stay,

| G |D |

   And I could be enough,   and we could be enough.

|Gadd2 |D   Gmaj7/D |D | ‖

   That would be e - nough.

Dear Theodosia

Words and Music by
Lin-Manuel Miranda

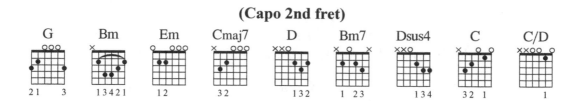

(Capo 2nd fret)

Intro |G |Bm |Em |Cmaj7 D ‖

Verse 1

‖ **G** |**Bm** |
Burr: Dear Theodosia, what to ____ say to you?
|**Em** |**Cmaj7**
   You have my eyes. You have your mother's name.
D |**G** |**Bm**
When you came into the world, you cried
                  |**Em** |**Cmaj7** **D** |
And it broke my ____ heart.
|**G** |**Bm** |
 I'm dedicating ev'ry ____ day to you.
|**Em** |**Cmaj7**
   Domestic life was never quite my style.
D |**G** |**Bm** |**Em**
When you ____ smile,   you knock me out, I fall a - part.
                  |**Cmaj7**
And I thought I was so ____ smart.

Pre-Chorus 1

D   ‖ G | Bm7
You will come of age with our young na - tion.
              | Em | Cmaj7
We'll bleed and fight for you, we'll make it right for you.
D | G | Bm7 | Em
If we lay a strong enough founda - tion we'll pass it on to you,
      | Cmaj7   D | G
We'll give the world to you, and you'll blow us all away,

Chorus 1

     ‖ Bm7 | Em |
Some - day, some   -   day.
| Cmaj7   D | G
   Yeah, you'll blow us all away,
     | Bm7 | Em | Cmaj7   D ‖
Some - day, some   -   day.

Verse 2

     ‖ G | Bm | Em
Hamilton: Oh, Philip, when you smile I am un - done.
   | Dsus4   D | G |
My ___ son.   Look at my ___ son.
| Bm | Em
 Pride is not the word I'm looking for.
          | Dsus4   D |
There is so much more inside me ___ now.
| G | Bm | Em
   Oh, Philip, you outshine the morning ___ sun.
   | Dsus4   D | G | Bm7 | Em
My ___ son.   When you ___ smile,   I fall a - part.
          | Dsus4   D   ‖
And I thought I was so ___ smart.

Bridge

        ‖ **C**   **D** |**C**   **D** |
Hamilton: My father wasn't around. **Burr:**   My father wasn't around.

         |**C**   **D** |**C**   **D** |
Hamilton: I swear that **Burr/Hamilton:** I'll be around ___ for __ you.

         |**C**   **D** |**Cmaj7**   **D** |
Hamilton: I'll do whatever it takes. **Burr:**   I'll make a million mistakes.

           |**Cmaj7**   **D** |**Cmaj7** |
Burr/Hamilton: I'll make the world safe and sound ___ for

    |**C/D**
You ____ will…

Pre-Chorus 2

           ‖ **G** |**Bm7**
Burr/Hamilton: Come of age with our young na - tion.

         |**Em** |**Cmaj7**
We'll bleed and fight for you, we'll make it right for you.

D |**G** |**Bm7**
If we lay a strong enough founda - tion

           |**Em**
    We'll pass it on to you.

         |**Cmaj7**   **D** |**G**
We'll give the world to you, and you'll blow us all away

Chorus 2

         ‖ **D** |**Em** |
Some - day, some - day.

|**Cmaj7**   **D** |**G** |**D**
    Yeah, you'll blow us all away, ___ some - day,

Bm7 |**Em** |**Cmaj7** |**G**   ‖
Some - day.

One Last Time

Words and Music by
Lin-Manuel Miranda

(Capo 3rd fret)

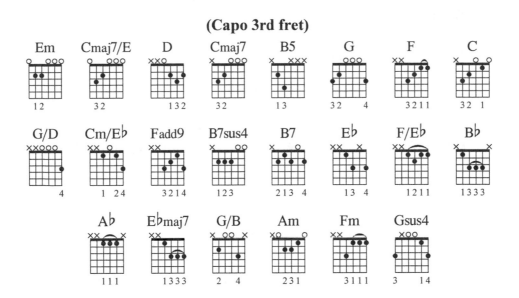

Verse 1

|**Em**   **Cmaj7/E** |**D**
Hamilton: *Mister President, you asked to see me.*

                                          |**Em**   **Cmaj7/E** |**D**
Washington: I know you're busy. **Hamilton**: *What do you need, sir?   Sir?*

                              |**Em**
Washington: I wanna give you a word of warning.

                                          Cmaj7/E
Hamilton: *Sir, I don't know what you heard,*

            |**D** |
But what - ever it is, Jefferson started it.

            |**Cmaj7** |**B5**
Washington: Thomas Jefferson resigned this morning.

                              ‖

Hamilton: *You're kidding.*

Verse 2

       |Em   Cmaj7/E

Washington: I need a favor.

                      |D

Hamilton: *Whatever you say, sir, Jefferson will pay for this behavior.*

          |Em   Cmaj7/E

Washington: Shh. ___ talk less!

                |D

Hamilton: *I'll use the press, I'll write under a pseudonym,*

                  |

You'll see what I can do to him.

        |Em   Cmaj7/E

Washington: I need you to draft an ad - dress.

            |D

Hamilton: *Yes! ___ He resigned. You can fin'lly speak your mind.*

           |Cmaj7 |B5

Washington: *No,*   he's stepping down so he can run for president.

                         |

Hamilton: *Ha! Good luck defeating you, sir.*

           |Cmaj7 |B5

Washington: I'm stepping down, I'm not running for president.

                  ||

Hamilton: *I'm sorry, what!*

          |G   F |

Chorus 1   **Washington**: One last time.

   | C   D |G   F |

   Relax, ___ have a drink ___ with me one last time.

   | C |D

   Let's take a break ___ to - night,

                  |Em   D

And then we'll teach 'em how to say goodbye,

C | G/D Cm/E♭   Fadd9 |G   D   C |

To say ___ good - bye,   you and ___ I

              |F   C   D

Hamilton: *No ___ sir, why?* **Washington**: I want to…

Verse 3

```
                  ‖ Em
Washington: Talk about neutrality.
                 Cmaj7/E                          | D
Hamilton: Sir, with Britain and France ____ on the verge of war,
                                        | Em                  Cmaj7/E
Hamilton: Is this the best time?
Washington:                    I wanna warn against partisan fighting.
Hamilton:                                              But…
                    | D
Washington: Pick up a pen, start writing.
              | Em                        Cmaj7/E
I wanna talk about what I have learned.
              | D
The hard won wisdom I have earned.
                            | Cmaj7                                    |
Hamilton: As far as the peo - ple are concerned, you have to serve,
| Em                  B7sus4                        B7      ‖
   You could contin  -  ue to serve. Washington: No!
```

Chorus 2

```
                   | G       F    |
Washington: One last time.
      |             C            D            |
          The peo - ple will hear ____ from me
| G       F    |             C         D
  One last time,   and if we get ____ this right,
                  | Em           D          | C    G/D
We're gonna teach 'em how to say goodbye,
Cm/E♭  Fadd9    G |   D   E♭  |
You        and     I.
```

Verse 4

                          | **F/E**♭   **E**♭   ‖**C**

Hamilton: *Mister President,* they will say you're weak.

                   |**B**♭ |

Washington: *No,*   they will see we're strong.

             |**C**

Hamilton: Your position is so unique.

                 |**B**♭ |

Washington: So I'll use it to move them along.

             |**C**

Hamilton: Why do you have to say goodbye?

                 |**B**♭ |**C**

Washington: If I say ____ goodbye the nation learns to move on.

                            |**F** **A**♭ | **B**♭ |

It outlives me when I'm gone.   Like the scripture says,

|**Em**   **D** |**C**   **G**

"Ev'ryone shall sit under their own vine and fig tree,

E♭**maj7**   **F** |**Em**

     And no one shall make them a - fraid."

                    D |**C**   **G** **D** |

They'll be safe in the nation we've __ made.

|**Em**   **D** |**C**

     I wanna sit under my own vine and fig tree.

G   **D** |**Em**

     A moment a - lone in the shade,

  D |**C** |**G**

At home in this nation we've made. One last time

                      |**F** |**G**   ‖

Hamilton: One last time.

Verse 5

‖ **N.C.** | |

Hamilton: *"Though, in reviewing the incidents of my administration,*

| | |

I am unconscious of intentional error, I am nevertheless too sensible

| |

Of my defects not to think it probable

|

That I may have committed many errors."

| **C**   **G/B**

Hamilton: I shall also carry with me the hope

Washington: The hope…

| **Am**   **Fm** |

Hamilton: *That my country will view them with in - dulgence; and that*

Washington: View them with in - dulgence…

| **C**   **G/B**

Washington: After forty five years of my life

Hamilton: *After forty five years of my life*

| **Fadd9**   **Fm**

Washinton: Dedi - cated to its service with an upright zeal,

Hamilton: *Dedi - cated to its service with an upright zeal,*

| **C**

Hamilton: *The faults of incompetent abilities will be*

| **Gsus4** |

Washington: Consigned to ob - livion, as I myself must soon be

Hamilton: *Consigned to ob - livion, as I myself must soon be*

| **G**   ‖

Washington: To the mansions of rest.

Hamilton: *To the mansions of rest.*

| **C**

Washington: I anticipate with pleasing expectation

Hamilton: *I anticipate with pleasing expectation*

| **B♭**

Washington: That re - treat in which I promise myself

Hamilton: *That re - treat in which I promise myself*

| **C**

Washington: To realize the sweet enjoyment of partaking,

Hamilton: *To realize the sweet enjoyment of partaking,*

| **B♭**

Washington: In the midst of my fellow citizens,

Hamilton: *In the midst of my fellow citizens,*

| **C**

Washington: The be - nign influence of good laws

Hamilton: *The be - nign influence of good laws*

| **B♭** | **F**

Washington: Under a free government, the ever fav'rite object of my heart,

Hamilton: *Under a free government, the ever fav'rite object of my heart,*

C | **B♭**   **F**

Washington: And the happy reward, as I ___ trust, of our mutual cares,

Hamilton: *And the happy reward, as I ___ trust, of our mutual cares,*

| **A♭** | **B♭**   ‖

Washington: Labors, and dangers.   One last time…

Hamilton: *Labors, and dangers.*

Outro

                   ‖ **C** |**B♭**

Woman: George Washington's going home.

                  Fadd9 |**C**

Hamilton: Teach 'em how to say ___ goodbye.

                          |**B♭**   **F** |

Ensemble: George Washington's going home. **Washington:** You and I!

              |**C** |**B♭**

Ensemble: George Washington's going home!

              F |**C**

Washington: Going home!

                        |**B♭**

Ensemble: George Washington's going home!

              F |**C**

Washington: History has ___ its eyes on you!

                       |**B♭**   **F**

Ensemble: George Washington's going home!

Washington: Yeah!

                  |**Am** |

Washington: We're gonna teach 'em how to say goodbye!

|**C** |**F** |

Teach 'em how to say goodbye! To say ___ goodbye! Say goodbye!

|**A♭** **N.C.**   **A♭** **B♭**   **C** |

One last time! Ensemble: One last   time!

            | **B♭** **F** **C** | | ‖

Ensemble: Time!

Hurricane

Words and Music by
Lin-Manuel Miranda

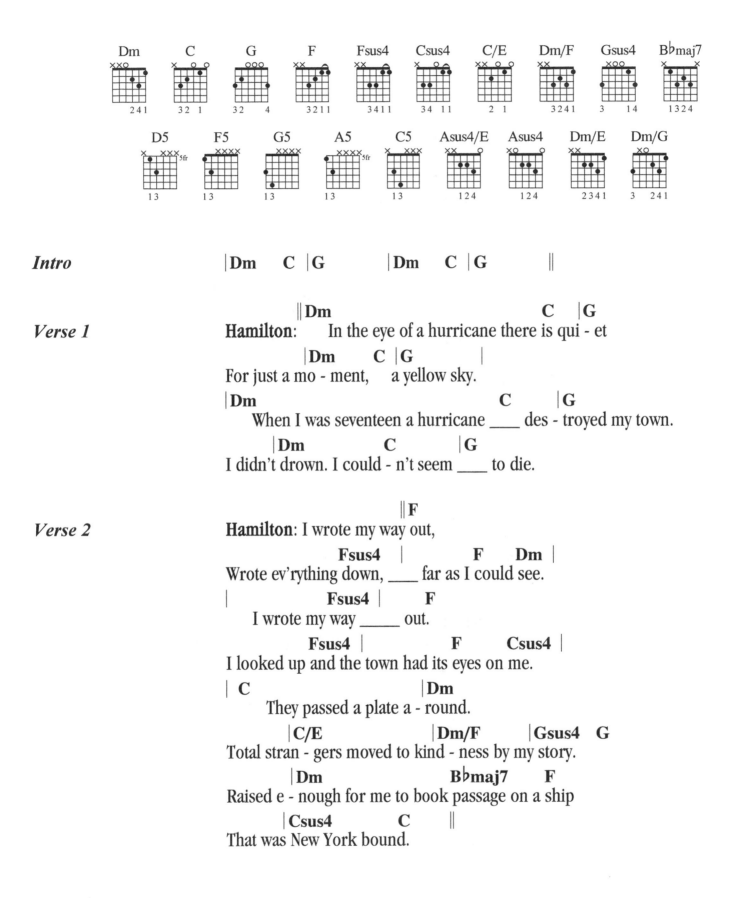

Intro

|Dm   C |G |Dm   C |G ||

Verse 1

‖Dm   C |G
Hamilton: In the eye of a hurricane there is qui - et

|Dm   C |G |
For just a mo - ment,   a yellow sky.

|Dm   C |G
    When I was seventeen a hurricane ___ des - troyed my town.

    |Dm   C |G
I didn't drown. I could - n't seem ___ to die.

Verse 2

                                ‖F
Hamilton: I wrote my way out,

        Fsus4 | F   Dm |
Wrote ev'rything down, ___ far as I could see.

| Fsus4 | F
    I wrote my way _____ out.

        Fsus4 | F   Csus4 |
I looked up and the town had its eyes on me.

| C |Dm
    They passed a plate a - round.

        |C/E |Dm/F |Gsus4 G
Total stran - gers moved to kind - ness by my story.

        |Dm   B♭maj7   F
Raised e - nough for me to book passage on a ship

        |Csus4   C ||
That was New York bound.

Verse 3

   ‖ **D5**   **F5**   **G5** |
I wrote my way out of hell. I wrote my way to revo - lution.

A5   **C5**   **D5**
I was louder than the crack in the bell.

         | **F5**   **G5**
I wrote E - liza love ___ letters until she fell.

         | **A5**   **C5**   **D5** |
I wrote a - bout the Constitution and de - fended it well.

| **F5**   **G5**
And in the face of ignorance and resis - tance,

 | **A5**   **C5**   **D5**
I wrote fi - nancial systems into exis - tence.

      | **F**
And when my prayers to God were met with indifference,

 | **Gsus4**   **G**   ‖
I picked up a pen, I wrote ___ my own deliverance.

Verse 4

      ‖ **Dm**   **C** | **G**
Hamilton: In the eye of a hurricane there is qui - et

         | **Dm**   **C** | **G** |
For just a mo - ment,   a yellow sky.

| **Dm**   **C** | **G**
    I was twelve when my mother died. ___ She was holding me.

              | **Dm**   **C** | **G**
We were sick and she was holding me. I could - n't seem ___ to die.

Bridge

      ‖ **Dm**
Burr: Wait for it, wait for it, wait for it.
                            | **Asus4/E**
Hamilton: I'll write my way out…

                                          |
Burr/Ensemble: Wait for it, wait for it, wait for it.
Hamilton: Write ev'rything down,
      | **Dm/F** | **Aus4**
Hamilton: Far as I can ___ see.
Burr/Ensemble: Wait for it, wait for it, wait for it, wait…
Eliza/Angelica
Mariah/Washington: His - to - ry   has   its…
                    | **Dm** |
Eliza/Angelica
Mariah/Washington: Eyes   on
Hamilton: I'll write my way out.
                   | **Dm/E** |
Hamilton: Overwhelm them with honesty.
Eliza/Angelica
Mariah/Washington: You…

Outro

      | **Dm/F**
Hamilton: This is the eye of the hurricane,
      | **Dm/G** |
This is the only way I can protect my legacy.
      | **Asus4** | **Dm**   ‖
Ensemble: Wait for it, wait for it, wait for it, wait…

Burn

Words and Music by
Lin-Manuel Miranda

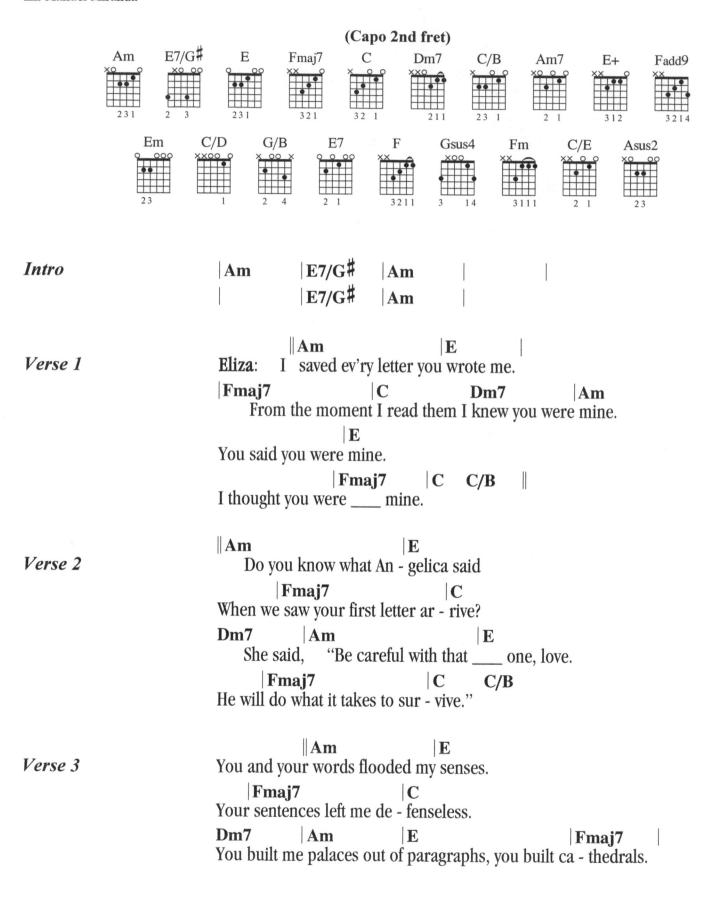

(Capo 2nd fret)

Intro

|Am |E7/G♯ |Am | |
| |E7/G♯ |Am |

Verse 1

‖Am |E |
Eliza: I   saved ev'ry letter you wrote me.
|Fmaj7 |C   Dm7 |Am
From the moment I read them I knew you were mine.
                |E
You said you were mine.
            |Fmaj7 |C   C/B   ‖
I thought you were ___ mine.

Verse 2

‖Am |E
Do you know what An - gelica said
        |Fmaj7 |C
When we saw your first letter ar - rive?
Dm7 |Am |E
She said,   "Be careful with that ___ one, love.
        |Fmaj7 |C   C/B
He will do what it takes to sur - vive."

Verse 3

‖Am |E
You and your words flooded my senses.
    |Fmaj7 |C
Your sentences left me de - fenseless.
Dm7 |Am |E |Fmaj7 |
You built me palaces out of paragraphs, you built ca - thedrals.

Verse 4

|C   C/B ‖Am |E
       I'm re - reading the letters you wrote me.

  |Fmaj7 |C   Dm7 |Am7
I'm searching and scanning for an - swers in every   line,

                   |E   E+ |Fmaj7 |
For some kind of sign, and when you were ___ mine

Chorus 1

| ‖C
    The world seemed ___ to...

  |Am |Em |Fadd9 |
Burn

|C |Am |Em |
 Burn.

Verse 5

|Fadd9   ‖Am |E
     You published the letters she wrote you.

 |Fmaj7 |C   C/D |Am
You told the whole world how you brought this girl into our   bed.

                |E |Fmaj7 |C C/D |
In clearing your name, you have ruined our ___ lives.

|Am |E |Fmaj7 |C
   Do you know what An - gelica said   when she read what you'd done?

Dm7 |Am7 |Em   E
  She said,   "You have married an Ic - arus.

   |Fadd9 |C
He has flown too close to the sun."

Verse 6

G/B   ‖Am |E7
You and your words, obsessed with your legacy.

   |Fmaj7   F |C
Your sentences border on senseless,

G/B |Am |E7 |Fmaj7
And you are paranoid in ev'ry paragraph how they per - ceive you.

     |
You, you, you...

Verse 7

```
     ‖Am                        |E
```
I'm e - rasing myself from the narrative.
```
     |Fmaj7          |C              Dm7
```
Let future historians wonder how E - liza
```
     |Am7                      |E            |
```
Re - acted when you broke her ___ heart.
```
|Fadd9                     |
```
   You have torn it all a - part,

Chorus 2

```
                 ‖C      |Am    |Em      |
```
I'm watching it   burn.
```
|Fadd9          |C      |Am      |
```
   Watching it   burn.
```
                          |
```

Verse 8

```
|Em     |Fadd9       Gsus4      ‖C
```
      The world has no right to my heart.
```
                       |E+
```
The world has no place in our bed.
```
     |Am7                    |Fmaj7
```
They don't get to know what I said.
```
     Gsus4       |C
```
I'm burning the memories,
```
            |E+                    |Am7
```
Burning the letters that might have re - deemed you.

Verse 9

```
         |Fmaj7 Gsus4       ‖C
```
You for - feit all rights to my heart.
```
                   |Fm
```
You forfeit the place in our bed.
```
     |Am7                  |Fadd9
```
You sleep in your office in - stead,
```
       Gsus4 |C                        |C/B      |
```
With only the memories of when you were ___ mine.
```
|C/E  C/D  C  |Fadd9       |
```
```
|N.C.              |Am      |E7/G♯ |Fmaj7  |C  Dm7  |Asus2     ‖
```
   I hope that you   burn.

It's Quiet Uptown

Words and Music by
Lin-Manuel Miranda

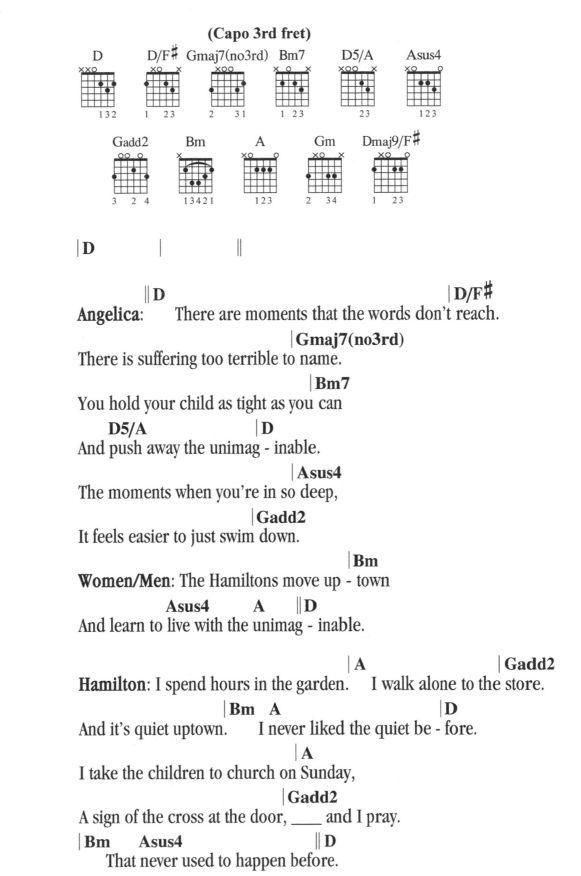

(Capo 3rd fret)

Intro |D | ‖

Verse 1

‖D |D/F♯
Angelica: There are moments that the words don't reach.

|Gmaj7(no3rd)
There is suffering too terrible to name.

|Bm7
You hold your child as tight as you can

D5/A |D
And push away the unimag - inable.

|Asus4
The moments when you're in so deep,

|Gadd2
It feels easier to just swim down.

|Bm
Women/Men: The Hamiltons move up - town

Asus4   A   ‖D
And learn to live with the unimag - inable.

Verse 2

|A |Gadd2
Hamilton: I spend hours in the garden.   I walk alone to the store.

|Bm A |D
And it's quiet uptown.   I never liked the quiet be - fore.

|A
I take the children to church on Sunday,

|Gadd2
A sign of the cross at the door, ___ and I pray.

|Bm   Asus4   ‖D
That never used to happen before.

Verse 3

                                       | A

Women: If you see him in the street, walking by himself,

                    | Gadd2

Talking to himself, have pity.

                                            | Bm

Hamilton: Philip, you would like it uptown. It's quiet uptown.

                  Asus4   **A**   **| D**

Women: He is working through the unimag - inable.

                              | A

Men: His hair has gone grey. He passes ev'ry day.

                                  | Gadd2

They say he walks the length of the city.

                                      | Bm

Hamilton: You knock me out, I fall apart.

                      Asus4   **A**   **| D**   **|**   **‖**

Company: Can you imag   -   ine?

Verse 4

                      ‖ D   **| Asus4**   **|**

Hamilton: Look at where we are.   Look at where we started.

| Gadd2   **|**

    I know I don't deserve you, Eliza.

| Bm   **Asus4**   **|**

    But hear me out.   That would be enough.

| D   **| Asus4**   **| Gadd2**

    If I could spare his life,   if I could trade his life for mine,

                                    | Bm

He'd be standing here right now ___ and you would smile,

Asus4   **A**   **‖**

    And that would be enough.

Verse 5

                      ‖ D   **| Bm**   **| D**

Hamilton: I don't pretend to know ___ the challenges we're fac - ing.

                              | Gadd2   **Gm**   **| D**

I know there's no replac - ing what we've lost ___ and you need time.

                          | Asus4   **|**

But I'm not afraid.   I know who I married.

| Gadd2   **| Bm**

    Just let me stay here by your side.

Asus4   **A**   **‖**

    That would be enough.

Verse 6

‖D |A

Women/Men: If you see him in the street, walking by her side,

                 |**Gmaj7(no3rd)**

Talking by her side, have pity.

                      |**Bm**

Hamilton: Eliza, do you like it uptown? It's quiet uptown.

       Asus4   **A** |**D**

Women/Men: He is try'ng to do the unimag - inable.

                  |**Asus4**

See them walking in the park, long after dark,

                 |**Gadd2**

Taking in the sights of the city.

                  |**Bm**

Hamilton: Look around, look around, Eli - za!

       Asus4   **A**   ‖**D**

Women/Men: They are try'ng to do the unimag - inable.

                       |**Dmaj9/F♯**

Verse 7   **Angelica:** There are moments that the words don't reach.

                |**Gadd2**

There's a grace too powerful to name.

                |**Bm**

We push away what we can never under - stand,

     |**Asus4**   **A** |**D**

We push a - way the uni - mag - inable.

              |**Asus4** |**Gadd2**

They are standing in the garden,   Alexander by Eliza's side.

              ‖

She takes his hand.

       ‖**Bm** **Asus4** |**D**

Verse 8   **Eliza:**   It's quiet up - town.

                               |

Women/Men(minus Hamilton): Forgiveness.

|**Asus4** |**Gadd2** |

  Can you imagine?   Forgiveness.

|**Bm**   **Asus4** **A**   ‖

  Can you i - mag - ine?

                     ‖**D** |

Outro   **Women/Men(minus Hamilton):**   If you see him in the street,

|**Asus4** |**Gadd2** |

  Walking by her side, talking by her side, have pity.

|**Bm**   **Asus4** |**D** | | ‖

  They are going through the unimag - inable.

STRUM & SING

The Strum & Sing series for guitar and ukulele provides an unplugged and pared-down approach to your favorite songs – just the chords and the lyrics, with nothing fancy. These easy-to-play arrangements are designed for both aspiring and professional musicians.

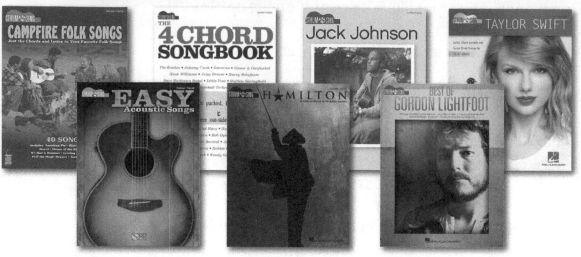

GUITAR

Acoustic Classics
00191891 ....$15.99

Adele
00159855 ....$12.99

Sara Bareilles
00102354 ....$12.99

The Beatles
00172234 ....$17.99

Blues
00159335 ....$12.99

Zac Brown Band
02501620 ....$19.99

Colbie Caillat
02501725 ....$14.99

Campfire Folk Songs
02500686 ....$15.99

Chart Hits of 2014-2015
00142554 ....$12.99

Chart Hits of 2015-2016
00156248 ....$12.99

Best of Kenny Chesney
00142457 ....$14.99

Christmas Carols
00348351 ....$14.99

Christmas Songs
00171332 ....$14.99

Kelly Clarkson
00146384 ....$14.99

Coffeehouse Songs for Guitar
00285991 ....$14.99

Leonard Cohen
00265489 ....$14.99

Dear Evan Hansen
00295108 ....$16.99

John Denver Collection
02500632 ....$17.99

Disney
00233900 ....$16.99

Eagles
00157994 ....$12.99

Easy Acoustic Songs
00125478 ....$19.99

Billie Eilish
00363094 ....$14.99

The Five-Chord Songbook
02501718 ....$12.99

Folk Rock Favorites
02501669 ....$14.99

Folk Songs
02501482 ....$14.99

The Four-Chord Country Songbook
00114936 ....$15.99

The Four Chord Songbook
02501533 ....$14.99

Four Chord Songs
00249581 ....$14.99

The Greatest Showman
00278383 ....$14.99

Hamilton
00217116 ....$15.99

Hymns
02501125 ....$8.99

Jack Johnson
02500858 ....$17.99

Robert Johnson
00191890 ....$12.99

Carole King
00115243 ....$10.99

Best of Gordon Lightfoot
00139393 ....$15.99

Dave Matthews Band
02501078 ....$10.95

John Mayer
02501636 ....$19.99

The Most Requested Songs
02501748 ....$14.99

Jason Mraz
02501452 ....$14.99

**Tom Petty –
Wildflowers & All the Rest**
00362682 ....$14.99

Elvis Presley
00198890 ....$12.99

Queen
00218578 ....$12.99

Rock Around the Clock
00103625 ....$12.99

Rock Ballads
02500872 ....$9.95

Rocketman
00300469 ....$17.99

Ed Sheeran
00152016 ....$14.99

The Six-Chord Songbook
02502277 ....$12.99

Chris Stapleton
00362625 ....$19.99

Cat Stevens
00116827 ....$17.99

Taylor Swift
00159856 ....$12.99

The Three-Chord Songbook
00211634 ....$12.99

Today's Hits
00119301 ....$12.99

Top Christian Hits
00156331 ....$12.99

Top Hits of 2016
00194288 ....$12.99

Keith Urban
00118558 ....$14.99

The Who
00103667 ....$12.99

Yesterday
00301629 ....$14.99

Neil Young – Greatest Hits
00138270 ....$15.99

UKULELE

The Beatles
00233899 ....$16.99

Colbie Caillat
02501731 ....$10.99

Coffeehouse Songs
00138238 ....$14.99

John Denver
02501694 ....$14.99

Folk Rock Favorites
00114600 ....$16.99

The 4-Chord Ukulele Songbook
00114331 ....$16.99

Jack Johnson
02501702 ....$19.99

John Mayer
02501706 ....$10.99

Ingrid Michaelson
02501741 ....$12.99

The Most Requested Songs
02501453 ....$14.99

Jason Mraz
02501753 ....$14.99

Pop Songs for Kids
00284415 ....$16.99

Sing-Along Songs
02501710 ....$15.99

HAL•LEONARD®

halleonard.com
Visit our website to see full song lists
or order from your favorite retailer.

*Prices, contents and availability
subject to change without notice.*